girl coming in for a landing

OTHER DELL YEARLING BOOKS YOU WILL ENJOY

DELL YEARLING BOOKS are designed especially to entertain and enlighten young people. Patricia Reilly Giff, consultant to this series, received her bachelor's degree from Marymount College and a master's degree in history from St. John's University. She holds a Professional Diploma in Reading and a Doctorate of Humane Letters from Hofstra University. She was a teacher and reading consultant for many years, and is the author of numerous books for young readers.

girl coming in for a landing

✖ a novel in poems ✖

April Halprin Wayland

illustrations by Elaine Clayton

A Dell Yearling Book

Published by
Dell Yearling
an imprint of
Random House Children's Books
a division of Random House, Inc.
New York

Visit us on the Web! www.randomhouse.com/teens

**Educators and librarians, for a variety of teaching tools,
visit us at www.randomhouse.com/teachers**

ISBN: 0-440-41903-4

Reprinted by arrangement with Alfred A. Knopf

Printed in the United States of America

March 2004

10 9 8 7 6 5 4 3 2 1

BVG

To my team—Gary and Jeff—
with so much love.

Your wings lift my words.

A.H.W.

For Simon.

E.C.

Contents

In Appreciation:

Many thanks

... to The Poetry Circle—especially Ruth Lercher Bornstein, Madeleine Comora, Ruth Feder, Joan Bransfield Graham, Peggy B. Leavitt, Hope Anita Smith, and Sonya Sones—for many productive popcorn mornings in Sonya's pink kitchen;

... to everyone at Knopf who helped to birth this book;

... to the amazing team (with a capital T!) of Lyra Halprin (my wonderful sister-sister-sister), Alan Jackson, Joshua Leahn Halprin Jackson, Julia Halprin Jackson, and Tam;

... to the dynamic duo of Saralee Halprin and Yo-Yo Ma Halprin;

... to Rosie, one of my best critics, and to Elsie and Snot;

... to the W. Sancington Trust and the Moonstone Arts Council;

... to Mrs. Tammy Clark and her students at Magruder Middle School in Torrance, California, for sharing their first-day-of-school thoughts;

... to the awesome Libby Moyer (the biggest heart in the beach cities);

... to my *faan* cousin, Marc-David Freed;

... to the late Myra Cohn Livingston, who encouraged me to write this book and who championed it for a long, long time.

Autumn

WRITING POETRY

In the middle of the night
I turn on my light

then slowly peel
off layers of me
with the press of each key.

ALL THIS SUMMER

All this summer
when I was alone,
I'd think about what he would say
and then he said it.

He did.

He'd walk with me hand in hand
in the late afternoons
along the sandbar of the Feather River.
He'd tell me, "You are the most important person in my life,"
and then he'd kiss my nose.

He would.

He'd pull leaves from my hair
and say, "Never leave me."
But I have. I've left him.
I've come back to school,
my two feet planted firmly on the ground.

I'm a teenager now.
I'll never walk with my invisible boyfriend again.

But I remember what he said.

JUST A FEW WORDS

I found a beautiful quote
by a writer, Luciano de Crescenzo.
Lou-chee-ON-oh wrote:

> *"We are each of us*
> *angels with only one wing,*
> *and we can only fly by embracing each other."*

Just a few words, but they make me
a little sad,
a little blue . . .

. . . as if I am striving for something higher,
trying to get off
the ground.

> But Lou,
> who
> will embrace *me*?

PERIOD.

It sounds so final.
Like things stop.
When you get it.

I know that when I finally get mine,
I'm going to be so thrilled I'm going to call it my
Exclamation Point.

LESLIE
MOVING BACK AFTER TWO YEARS

You've been away so long—
when you knock on my front door,
will I recognize your soft eyes?

Did you miss me?
I missed giggling with you walking home.
I missed your soft, soft eyes.

Do you remember the day we set out nuts for the birds
and kept moving them closer to my open door,
finally into the living room?

Do you remember
how we closed the door,
trapping a blue jay?

Do you remember what he did to the piano,
and how we laughed because we didn't know what to do with him
once we had him inside?

YOU KNOCK! I'm afraid—I'm excited—
I take a breath before I open the door . . .
maybe a bird will fly in.

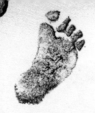

SEPTEMBER—SANTA MONICA

Mom and I
pull on our yellow wool sweaters,
grab the leash, call Peanuts,
and go for a search on the beach.

Just us,
a slice of moon in the blue above,
and Peanuts sniffing the air,
waggling his stubby tail wildly.

Me and Mom
on the prowl:
our scarved heads,
our backs bent down,

hands behind,
intent
amid the piles of shells
swarming on the sand.

Our own beach,
ours alone.
Just us and the gulls
and the wash of the shells.

On the prowl
for moonstones.

WHEN I WAS SMALL

When I was small,
I didn't want my old stuffed cat, Harold.
I wanted your elegant dog, Ariel Sibel.

I didn't want
my dumb name.
I wanted your beautiful one.

When I was small,
I wanted to be like you—
tall.

I wanted to be the older sister.
I still sometimes
want to be you.

Did you
ever want to be
me?

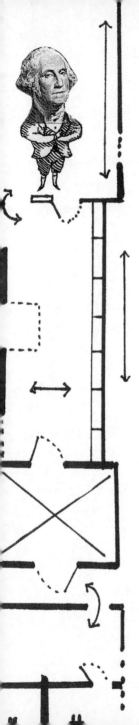

BACK TO SCHOOL
LAST YEAR

Last year
I worried about where the rooms were
and all   those   kids.

I didn't know
what kind of binder to buy *(three-ring?)*
or how much lunch money to bring.

Last year I got my hair cut the day before school
   started.
Dumb me.
It was way   too   short that first day.

And last year I didn't know if I should buy new jeans
or if my comfortable overalls would be dorky . . .
or even if anyone cared.

Last year I wasn't sure what time to set my alarm.
Last year
I was *scared*.

BACK TO SCHOOL
THIS YEAR

This year
I've got the perfect organizer
with pockets for every subject (except PE).

This year
I ironed my lavender shirt three days ago
and laid everything out last night.

This year
I set the alarm for six forty-five:
just right.

This year
I got my hair cut two weeks ago
so that it is *exactly* the right length today.

This year
I have Mr. C for science,
Mr. Barton from Tennessee for language arts

and Ms. Konigsberg
for chorus.
Again.

Last year I worried: Who was I? What did I know?
This year
I put on glitter Chap Stick and *go*!

PRAYER

I pretend I'm not looking for Carlo in the crowded hall.

I walk by without recognizing him.
(He got a haircut, too.)

I hear his voice
and turn.

My heart flickers.
It says, *"This year. This year."*

FIRST PERIOD, FIRST DAY

Here I am in first period language arts
in my ironed lavender shirt.
Mr. Barton, new this year,
ambles toward the back of the quiet classroom
in cowboy boots, passing out questionnaires.
The blue papers come my way in waves.

Yen-Mei hands me one.
Her brows gather together as she reads the questions.
It is five pages asking what do we think the most important qualities in a
teacher are what are our favorite books-movies-TV programs whether we like to
write where we like to sit in a class who our best friend is and more.
I let out a sigh, take a deep breath, and dive down into this
familiar lagoon.

I haven't swum here since summer started,
this place where we are all treading water just over our desks,
diving down to rummage around
pulling things up from the deep
and placing them on the page
until he says,

"Pens down, y'all. Eyes up here."
Oh yes.
I remember.
We're
back.

WHEN DAD COMES HOME

When he is driving down five hundred miles,
my heart thumps wildly—jumps all day at school.
My friends say, "Whoa, you sure are full of smiles."
I tingle. I disguise it. I act cool.
I barely notice balls as they whiz past.
I run the halls, I slide, I break the rules.
I need something to chew—I need it fast.
I bite my nails, I nibble on my hair.
Then Yen-Mei asks how long an earthquake lasts.
My legs are shaking wildly on her chair.

At three I'm home to set an extra plate,
though it's not close to supper, it's my wish,
but I know he'll be really, really late.
His plate's still there. I dry my dinner dish.
I brush my teeth and get in bed soooo slooooooow . . .
when Mom leans down and whispers her g'night,
I hear the groan of the garage door low—
he's home! Leap out of bed, snap on the light
and fling the back door open—
"*Hi! Hello!*"

I DIDN'T KNOW
HOW MUCH MY FATHER KNEW

Today after school,
he walks with me all the way to Palisades Park.
I tell him all I know about the scientist Mendel,
about inherited traits,
sweet peas,
fruit flies,
and everything else Mr. C said.

He tells me all he knows
about dominant and recessive,
about blondes and brunettes,
about people who can curl their tongues
(my dad and I can)
and those who can't
(my mom and my sister can't).

It's so amazing.
Daddy and me
on the same page
on the same subject
on the same sidewalk
to the ocean
and back.

I didn't know
how much my father knew.

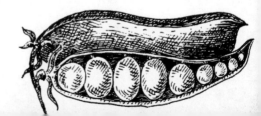

HEALER

You walk into class—
my head clears.

No kidding.
You are my aspirin.

CRUSH X 2

An odd pair:

Frank—all dramatic with wild, shaggy hair.
Carlo is calmer—combed with care.

Carlo's laid-back.
Frank wisecracks.

Carlo waits.
Contemplates.

Frank is an actor and proud.
Loud.

Carlo plays cello. He's mellow.
Frank's full of drama and trauma.

Carlo sits back and admires.
Frank sets figurative fires.

When Frank roars, Carlo's eyes glimmer.
Frank boils over; Carlo simmers.

An odd pair
an interesting blend . . .

how can I choose between
two best friends?

MR. C EXPLAINS
THE DOUBLE HELIX

when   when
          your
father   mother
          met
          your
father   mother
    he   she
      thought
    he   she
  would make a
       great
mother   father

FRANK

The bell rings.
He asks if I will listen
yes oh yes yes yes
I can hardly hear him.
He tells me, straight to my eyes,
of Cathy who died
and how he loved her so
long ago.

I am smarter than my breathing,
sitting on the cold metal banister
in the after-school hallway.
I wonder
if Cathy is really dead
or just in his head . . .
But oh
how I yes inside.

WHAT THEY MEAN WHEN THEY SAY THAT
BLOOD IS THICKER THAN WATER

When Great-Aunt Ida asked me
to send her some of that thick red fabric
you can only get on the Santa Monica Promenade
                if it wouldn't be too much trouble,

I went to the fabric store,
found a box for it,
and walked it to the post office.

When Great-Aunt Ida asked me
to please tape
that sewing program on the radio
                if it wouldn't be too much to ask,

I found a tape to tape over,
remembered to record it,
packed it in bubble wrap, and sent it to her.

Once a month I ride the bus
to Great-Aunt Ida's little apartment
and help her shop

for hat feathers,
sewing supplies,
and those great-tasting vitamin Cs from the
    health food store.

There is something about Great-Aunt Ida
and her fabric scraps,
and trying on her handmade hats.

Even when I get my
going-home-from-Great-Aunt-Ida's headaches,
I get a kick out of her.

Or at least most of me does
most
of the time.

TAKING VIOLIN

I open my case
tighten my bow
pluck a string to tune.
I love to listen to it chirp across the echoing room.

My friends are in class
reading about
a famous English king,
but I am training this wooden bird upon my arm to sing.

POETRY IS MY UNDERWEAR

My sister found them.

Read them out loud.
She's so proud,

she's running to our parents
waving my poems in the air.

Doesn't she know
she's waving my *underwear*?

SISTER

Sometimes
I want the insides of my drawers
to be as orderly as yours.

Other times
I want to sweep my arm
across your shelves

dumping all of your carefully lined-up stuffed animals
and alphabetized books
into one big messy pile on the floor.

IMPRINTING

Today Mr. C told us
about this scientist who pushed a vacuum cleaner
past a brood of ducklings
just as they were hatching
and how after that,
those ducklings followed the vacuum cleaner
everywhere—
nearly glued to it.

Imprinting, he called it.

Which made me think
about last year
that first day of school
and how
I must have been
hatching
just as Carlo
walked past.

WHY I AM A LOT LIKE A HORSE

When Ox was interested,
really *interested* in me,
I was annoyed.
He'd wait for me after orchestra, he'd find me at lunch,
and once he gave me a science fiction book that he loved.

I hate science fiction.

But I just read a book by a guy who trains horses.
He says that if he moves toward the horse,
looks it in the eye,
and squares his body straight at the horse,
it retreats.

If the man stops,
looks disinterested,
moves his body
into a less threatening position,
the horse advances.

It's like Ox.
And me.
When he was falling all over himself
to be with me,
I wanted to flick him away with my tail.

But lately
he's been hanging around
a girl who plays clarinet.
And lately I have missed
being annoyed.

SHE SEES THINGS

"Tonight's moon
looks like the Cheshire Cat,"
Leslie says. She sees things.
She finds things:

"Look at this color,
look at it,"
Leslie says,
holding up a piece of rusty tin.

So today on the way home from school,
I find a flattened bottle cap.
I see its lizard-blue belly exposed.
I save it for her.

Leslie sprinkles my path
with wonders
under the grin
of the moon.

GREAT-AUNT IDA

She is hunched over,
crunched up,
bent
like an empty soda can.

How does it feel,
I wonder,
to be shaped
like a lowercase *r*?

How does it feel
to have to raise your head up to the counter
when you speak to Ramon, the bank teller?

She is hunched over,
crunched up,
bent
like an empty soda can,

waiting
to be recycled.
I wish
I could straighten her.

PREPARING FOR THE AUDITION

She says,
"Lift your chin, stand tall."
She's helping me work out
this fourteen-line tangle of words
that doesn't make sense
at all.

Every night after supper
she directs from the stool by the stove:
"Project,
let it flow,
e-*nun*-ciate,
go slow."

It's hard
to repeat and repeat every night
but I love being warmed by this circle of heat
from Mom and the kitchen light
as I prepare
for my brave day.

MY VERSION OF WILLIAM SHAKESPEARE'S "SONNET NUMBER TWELVE"

When I do count the clock that tells the time
And see my whole day gone and all its light;
When I sort out this sonnet's classic rhyme
And try to comprehend with all my might;
When it occurs to me that I'll be teased
By fellow students after they have heard
My sonnet said upon these trembling knees,
My fervent wish? That I'm disguised (with beard).
Then of *my* wisdom do I question make.
What was I thinking when I said I'd try
For Drama Club—was I not yet awake?
Now I must climb from this black hole hereby;
For nothing 'gainst Mr. J can make defense
Save bribes, to brave him when he hears me hence.

AUDITIONING FOR DRAMA CLUB

It's been a big eighteen-wheeler idling in my bedroom.
It ran its huge wheels over my whole life,
from the minute I woke
until I finished my homework and sank into bed,
leaving its tire prints over my pillow each night.

The day has finally come.
I walk into the drama room,
that big diesel snorting behind me.
When my name is called, I walk onto the stage ready—
ready to recite Will's "Sonnet Number Twelve."

There are only a few here:
Mr. J
and the other kids who are auditioning.
I look out at them
and see nothing.

I look inside
and say Will's words
as if it were one of those nights in the kitchen
when I practiced making their meaning
clear.

I am sweating.
The fourteen lines are over.
I feel like a wide open road
as that truck shifts gears
and finally disappears.

WRITER: CREATOR

I want to
make something
                    beautiful.

Peaches.

If I could
make peaches—grow them
from my pen . . .

or stretching my palms
up to the sun, watch as
they grow from my lifeline,

that
would be something
                    beautiful.

ALONE

Quote, I wouldn't be caught dead at a dance, unquote,
Frank said to Carlo.
Carlo agreed.

Which leaves me

because Leslie's away
and Yen-Mei has to stay
with her brother.

Bother.

Which leaves me alone
but I'm not
staying home.

THOSE SCHOOL DANCES

At the dance,
I wander into the
cold-tiled bathroom:
fixing, fixing, a line
of fixing girls,
making sure.
What's wrong?
Is it the color of my lipstick?
Is that why I'm not being asked to dance?
Is it my bitten fingernails?

I wander back to the fringe
of the cool gym
to heat my wall spot.
Other wall-warmers
are whisked away.
I work hard, hiding my fingertips
from inspection.

I leave
slowly
when the lights flash on,
collecting a balloon for my room
and confetti to sprinkle in my hair;
go out into the chill night
to watch for that bronze Buick's headlights blazing
and my father's
bathrobed figure
in the driver's seat.

Back home,
I cuddle up to comfortable
bodies on a queen-size
bed, watch a mystery movie, and hold my mother's
warm
and bitten
fingertips.

AFTER EVERYONE
GOES TO SLEEP

This computer
pulls long lines of letters from me.
Birthing.

Each word
slides out
slowly

I am tired
I should shut this off and go to sleep
but each insistent sentence

yells, "Here I am!"
and I can only tell what I am feeling
by reading

these long lines of letters
still damp
as they emerge.

Winter

MR. BARTON

I like him.
I like all the stuff he teaches
about "The Waste Land."
I like that line, "April is the cruelest month."
But I don't think he reads our assignments.

Mr. Barton is also the track coach,
he plays the fiddle,
he's a minister for a church in Malibu,
he has two little kids *and* he's an English teacher.

But
I don't think
he reads our work.
And I worked *hard*
on this one.

So—in the middle of my paper
I type up a page that looks exactly like all the other pages.
It has paragraphs.
And quotation marks every once in a while.
And footnotes.

But this page
isn't about English.
This page
is a recipe
for fruitcake.

SEVEN MINUTES OF HEAVEN

Bill Berkmeyer
is on our guest list
because he is one year older,
because he is Yen-Mei's friend,
and because he knows how to kiss.

So when we play Seven Minutes of Heaven
in the backyard and it's my turn,
I put my hand in the hat,
pull out a folded slip of paper,
and open it. It says "Bill."

He takes me to the dark side of the house
where the vines grow thick.
I swallow hard.
"I've never really *kissed* a guy before," I say.
"Can you teach me?"

So he tells me to tilt my neck back a little more
and to sort of swirl my tongue around his.
Our noses are so close—
is mine going to bump his?
Do I have bad breath?

I taste cigarette smoke and chocolate chip cookies.
I kind of like the swirling part
I'm amazed that our faces fit together
that we don't bump noses
that we can both breathe.

When I remember
to breathe.
I like it
and
I feel I'm learning a lot.

43

WAITING FOR WAFFLES

The TV talks in the other room,
the ironing board stands, hands on hips,
in the middle of Great-Aunt Ida's kitchen

and I sit in the burgundy booth
in my pj's as
Great-Aunt Ida makes waffles.

I love pouring batter onto the waffle iron.
It's like writing poems—
from puddles to patterns.

If I stare at the black light
willing it to turn red . . .
it takes forever.

Just like writing. Sometimes I have to
not write
in order to write.

So I slide around
the vinyl seat
to look out her second-story window

at the birds.
I am waiting
for waffles.

SAVIOR

Frank Constantino
snuck into science lab,
stole all the snails,
and set them free.

We could not do
our science experiments
and everyone thought
that Frank was weird.

Everyone
except
the snails.
And me.

MY FATHER WHISTLES THE HILLS

In the bare light of the stars,
my father is driving home.
I am raking my hair with a comb;
my father is whistling out there.

He whistles high for the hills,
trills low for canyons.
He follows the natural notes of the land, and
the wheel moves in his hands.

While I stare into the mirror,
somewhere my father
is whistling nearer,
                    nearer.

ride

CARLO'S LAP

Laughing, tonight, after Christopher's party,
we pile into Yen-Mei Chen's stepfather's car.

"No room at the inn," I say softly to Leslie,
and even the kids in the front turn and grin.

We squeeze in.
The door slams shut.
I'm shoved on
Carlo's lap!

> *words / stick*
> *clocks / stop*
> *blood / goes / cold*

The car moves.

Part of my brain still works.
It prays

> *never*
> *let this*
> *car ride*
> *end.*

DADDY DOING DISHES

Who wants
to wake up to dirty dishes?
No one now, no one now

Daddy
especially,
so he'll do them now, do them now

The kitchen light shines
right on his head
the rest of us are all in bed

Thirsty, glass in hand,
I stand in the doorway—
stand and stand

He whistles Mama's music low,
no radio
he takes so long, he washes slow

and me, I lean against the door
and watch his back
until my father turns off the water.

The room is quiet. No sound.
I don't know whether to let out my breath or stay,
spellbound.

He doesn't turn around.
No—
with a low birdcall

he reaches for a towel.
Because Daddy doesn't like to wake up
to any dishes at all.

AT THE BUS STOP

I see Yen-Mei
wearing gray,
her mauve skirt long.

My rainbow colors
now seem

        wrong.

FAAN POWMS

Mr. Barton asks me to stay after class today.
My hand shakes zipping up my backpack.
What did I do wrong?

"Your lines of poetry,"
he says in that beautiful drawl,
"are so *faan*."

"You are writing on a *haa-er* level,
and I want you to think seriously
about getting your *powms* published."

Is there a floor beneath my feet?
He hands me a list,
"Where Can a Young Writer Get Published?"

Firecrackers! Electric guitars! Whipped cream!
Roller coasters!
Carlo!

This is definitely
one of the best days
of my life.

I'm boarding a plane
I'm flying
all the way down this hall.

OUIJA BOARD

"Place OUIJA® talking board upon the laps of two persons
facing each other, lady and gentleman preferred. Place
OUIJA® mysterious message indicator in center of OUIJA®
talking board resting fingers with the least possible pressure
upon the mysterious message indicator, allowing it to move
freely over OUIJA® talking board in all directions."

Leslie and I close our eyes.
"Go ahead and ask it a question," she whispers.
A chill shivers up between my shoulder blades.
There is, after all, only one question.
"Who loves me?" I whisper,
then rest my fingers with the least possible pressure
upon the mysterious message indicator,
allowing it to move freely
in all directions.
It's hard to stay absolutely absolutely still.
My fingertips quiver.
Don't breathe.
Don't.
Breathe.
Nothing's happening.
We sit knee to knee in my bedroom
waiting.
Forever.
And then—it begins.

Is it sliding on its own?
Or am I moving it?
It floats across the board like a ghost.

I feel as if we are dancing, this ghost and I.
It's leading me somewhere. I can tell.
I hope.
It stops.
My eyes open. Leslie is leaning forward—her eyes are open, too.
"Is that a *C*?" she whispers.
I lean over and look into the mysterious message indicator's
    plastic porthole.
"I think it is," I whisper.
"It is," she says, sitting back again and closing her eyes.
I close my eyes, ready for the ride.
Away it glides, slipping across the alphabet.
My fingertips quiver.

JUST HANGING OUT

You came dragging home
from school today
and just hung out with me.
Just us.

Two sisters hanging out.
We listened to music in your room—
you worked on your quilt spread out on the rug,
I worked on a poem.

The sun poured in.
And then you said the nicest thing.
You said:
"This is great.

Sometimes I forget about anyone but

                                        me
                                        me
                                        me

and miss all the
you you you
jumping around
in this crazy life."

And I said,
"I was just thinking
the exact
same thing,"

and then
I nearly
hugged
you.

AN AUTHOR
CAME TO SCHOOL TODAY

An author came to school today
and listened as one by one,
we read our poems.
I lost my place
and had to start over.

The author read a book to us—
her book—
bound and solid.
Frank passed me a note.
"She has fish lips," it said.

You could say she did.
But then she said,
"I began writing
when I was a teenager."
Like me.

The author
left her book for us
and when Frank left,
I went up
and touched it.

MOOD

I bristle like a bottlebrush today.

Wherever I turn,

I scratch.

Beware!

DRAMA

After school
        in the drama room,
Mr. J directs a scene.

I stand draped
        in the doorway,
                violin case against my calf,
                        eyes glued to the stage.

Behind,
        behind the doorway
                and my violin case
                        and me,
        a shadow builds.
I don't move.

There is room to pass by.

Instead, Carlo stands in the doorway
which frames us like a puzzle:
almost interlocking.

My eyes
are glued
to the scene.

My thigh
        is brushed
                by his.

I breathe out.

DUET

Yen-Mei plays duets
With me: a game of chase!

And neither one of us
Can keep a serious face.

Our fingers, in allegro,
Fly across the strings!

(In the presto passages
It seems our bows are wings!)

The notes rush by—I'm keeping up—
And then I miss a few.

She bursts out laughing when I say,
"Okay—so where *are* you?!?"

We settle down, I hold my breath.
And then she nods: my bow

Begins adagio.
Mozart melts upon my strings,

And then he melts on hers.
I close my eyes—breathe in the song,

Which all around me stirs.
I feel it deep, it lights my soul . . .

We glow.

PROCRASTINATION

Ancient dogs
circled in the grass
round and round
to tamp it down

I am dog
circling, too
round and round
as all dogs do

round my homework
round my desk
finally working
then I rest.

REHEARSAL

This music is so
amazing, it builds a nest
of tears in my throat.

SCIENCE HOMEWORK

Mr. C gives each of us a different plant,
saying, "Find out what its Latin name is."

Groan. I'll bet this red flower's name is
Homework toomuchus.

Okay, fine—I'm a detective,
searching for a missing person.

Figuring out her family
narrowing down her name

groping for her group
by the number of leaves

by the shape of the flower
by the shape of my brain

                              which is fried.

The *Jepson Manual: Higher Plants of California*
points to *Penstemon.*

It's past midnight when I go on-line
and find—the *Penstemon* Web site!

Hurray! This flower by my computer
has a name: *Penstemon centranthifolius!*

I'm a private investigator.
I've tracked down the missing person.

Tomorrow I bring her back to Mr. C,
alive.

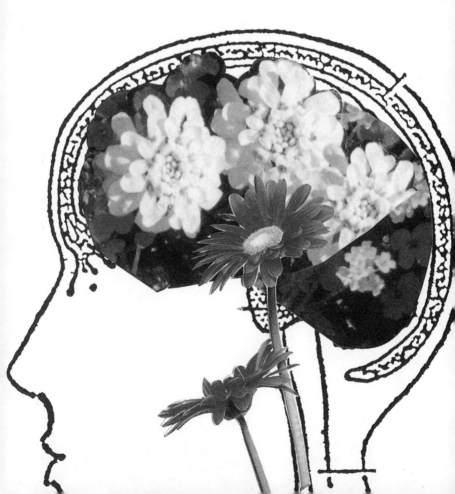

I WALK BESIDE GREAT-AUNT IDA

My hand is on her back—
we are dancers on a dance floor

the man's light touch
telling the woman where to slide, when to turn.

She describes the dentist who damaged her gums last July,
the hats she designed in her twenties,

the orphanage food
when she was five,

as I guide her away
from pieces of broken sidewalk.

IT'S PERFECTLY CLEAR

Leslie called me "unsupportive."
She said I didn't help her
make campaign posters on Friday.

Leslie called *me* "unsupportive."
She said she'd made it perfectly clear
she needed help on Friday.

Leslie called me
"unsupportive."
She *hadn't* made it clear.

Leslie
was a jerk
on Friday.

BIG ARGUMENT
WITH LESLIE

Arguing
Is strange.
The thing we are climbing
Becomes B R I T T L E.

One of us falls,
Then the other,
Shouting
As we drop.

Angrily
Blaming,
Loud;
Deaf.

In falling,
In the darkness,
At least there are
Words

Shouted up—
At least we are glaring
Into each other's
Eyes

At least
We are trying
To crash into each other
As we fall.

CURSING LESLIE

May rats scurry under your bed!
May rotting hot dogs smell up your refrigerator!

May a never-ending car alarm shatter your sleep before finals!
May you have infinite pimples and a double chin!

And may there be a cat litter box in your room
that you can never find!

READY TO WAKE THESE BIRDS

At night
the birds are still near,
just have to know that they are.
Can feel their black wings glisten,
can hear their hushed breathing,
can close my eyes and see them
sleeping all around.

At night
when I feel so empty,
so little in a dark room,
so tired after so much sleep,
just have to know that our friendship
flying against this moonless night
is ready to wake these birds,
come morning.

I HAVE TO WRITE

I have to write.
A splinter pushes up through my skin
and I can't sleep
until this sliver of words
works its way out.

AFTER AN ARGUMENT

I never stay in the room long enough
when other people argue
to know the *after*.
But now I can guess:

you both land,
clunk,
just miss the pillows,
a little bruised.

But somehow it works out,
it's okay,
you both land on your bottoms,
the pillows go back on the bed.

You both look pretty silly . . .
really silly.
So I guess after,
maybe there's laughter.

GRAND CENTRAL MARKET,
LOS ANGELES

Mom took us out of school (out of *school*!)
To drive through shadowed canyons
Between tall buildings
To Grand Central Market!

To taste Mexican candy
That melts sweet milk down your throat,
To pick out cactus fruit and octopus,
Smell giant fish on ice,

See kosher chickens hanging upside down,
Chew fantastic dried figs from bins.
Biting into our own special day
And a good pastrami sandwich,

We could barely keep up
With her sandals sweeping the sawdust aside
In the middle of the week
In the middle of a day

In *Grand Central Market* in downtown L.A.!

FAT CURSE

I hate the boys
in the front of the bus
who tease that girl.
They call her Shamu, the whale.

I walk by
and look at them menacingly.
Inside I think:
I am putting a curse on you:

One day,
you will be fat.
You won't be able
to stop eating.

You will remember
this bus,
the girl,
and me.

One day,
you won't be able to stop
eating
your words.

FAN

I know you.

I see you eating two vanilla wafers
every day at the end of lunch.

I know your bulky black jacket.

I swear I can separate your footsteps
in the crowded hallway.

Let me in, let me in.

DRIVING THAT DOG CRAZY

When Mr. C teaches science,
he tells us stories.

When he was a boy on his way to school,
he'd tease a big, mean dog

by dragging a stick
against her fence.

One day,
dragging that stick *tic-tic-tic,*

driving that dog to a barking frenzy,
he came to the gate

that was always closed
but this day it stood

WIDE
OPEN.

Today Mr. C teaches us about
adrenaline.

INTERESTING . . .

When I send in my heart
—my poetry—
to a publisher,
it's called submitting.

Spring

SPRING BREAK

The best clouds in the business
      are right above me
right now.

We're riding in this teal blue convertible
      those clouds just dozing
      in about forty-nine different shapes
      white as clean paper,
      their edges like feathers against the blue sky,
blue as Dad's eyes.

Dad drives, my sister's in front
      I lay my head on Mom's lap in the back.
      I lay my head on her lap
      as he drives this teal blue convertible
      that we rented special
just for these four days in Albuquerque.

In it, we are open to the whole world
      to the whole sky
      and I know right now
      I can *see*
      that these are
the best clouds in the business.

POOH

Carlo's coming to my party on Saturday!
I look around my room
These walls *need* something

What was it he said?
How much he liked . . . what children's book was it?
Winnie-the-Pooh?

He told me how profound it was,
How philosophical, "A work of genius," he said
I run to the library

Find the book
Skim it while I
Xerox the pictures

Wish I had time to read about this silly old bear
Mount the pictures on colored paper
Put them on my wall

On Saturday, he checks out my room
"Ah," he says, ". . . *Winnie-the-Pooh* . . ."
(I wait) "Isn't that book brilliant?"

I look in his black eyes
And realize
He doesn't remember telling me about it.

I am relieved.
I look in his black eyes
And realize he isn't as brilliant as I thought he was

Silly old bear.
But still—I'll keep the pictures up
All year.

SPIN THE BOTTLE

spin the bottle
on my front lawn
my bare feet were freezing
so I've got socks on

spin the bottle
go, baby, go
I pray it stops in front of
divine Carlo

he takes me in his arms
and kisses me hard
I can't believe it's happening
in my front yard

I WONDER WHY

he stopped
in the middle

of kissing me passionately on the lips
to give my neck a nip.

Beth said he didn't move aside her coat
to kiss *her* throat

when her spin
stopped at him.

I wonder why
he kissed my lips / neck / lips? What did it signify?

Was it a whim?
Just a dumb spin-the-bottle turn to him?

Was my breath so bad
that he just had to take a break?

Did he think I was a flake?
Was it a hair?

Or—
did he care?

Was he just being polite?
Or did he really want to kiss
        just me all night?

ALL I CAN THINK ABOUT

All I can think about is
kissing him.

All I can write about
in notes passed to Leslie

is kissing
and she replies

about kissing
and more.

All I can think about is
kissing him

and more.

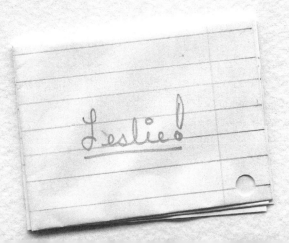

FANTASY BEFORE THE SPRING DANCE

Here's my chance:
to be someone else
just for tonight.

To be someone who
wears this dress,
arrives in style,

walks in owning the room.
Someone drop-dead gorgeous.
Someone Not Me.

Just for tonight.
Please, God:
don't let my parents pick me up in a pumpkin.

ONE MINUTE

Mr. Barton said, "Write in your journals every night
for one minute. By the clock."
He said this forces us to focus.

Today Leslie, Yen-Mei, Frank, Carlo, and I
met at lifeguard station five.
We flew kites in the fog until

it looked
as if we had the sky
on a string.

We had a kite war,
and a kite funeral.
We built a sand castle,

watched the sunset,
and walked up the hill
to Yen-Mei's for hot chocolate.

So tonight I wrote for one minute
about when we were digging tunnels
in the wet sand,

and Carlo's hand
touched mine.
An accident?

Our eyes met
over a turret.
Did I imagine it?

I feel
like a kite
in the fog.

PERIOD!

Period:
an interval of time that is meaningful in the life of a person

Welcome to my meaningful interval!

I feel
meaning-full
beautiful
      audible
Sitting Bull
(Sitting Bull?)
      laudable
notable
terrible
      powerful
worshipful
sensible
      sorrowful
changeable
fanciful
      WONDERFUL

Welcome to my wonderful interval!

TWO GREAT THINGS

He walked me to orchestra today.
This is the first time he's walked me to a class on purpose—
we weren't just in the hall, going the same way.

My legs felt Not Mine.
I was aware of the spacing of his paces.
I focused on keeping up.

Then he announced,
"I like what you said at lunch about hate crimes."
He liked what I said.

Two Great Things at once.

I didn't know he was listening to us at lunch (!)
which is a good thing. Because I was on *fire*;
I have a lot to say about hate crimes—

but when Carlo appears,
my brain goes in my lunch sack,
and my lunch sack gets tossed in the trash.

If I had known he was listening at lunch, I would have
   opened my mouth
and out would have come
garbage.

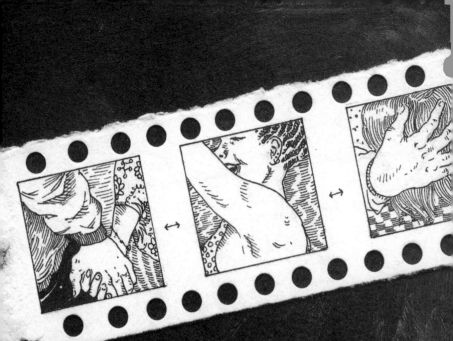

HE ASKS ME OUT

He walks me to class again,
looks sideways at me
and starts:
"Would you like to—"

He doesn't have a chance
to finish
my words trip over his . . .
"Yes!"

FREE SAMPLE

Mom got a fancy women's shaver in the mail
and gave it to me.

I tucked it away in my underwear drawer
to save for a special occasion

which is here:
he asked me out.

First,
a lavender bubble bath.

Next, honeysuckle shampoo
and conditioner.

Then, I slather my legs with
baby powder–scented shaving cream

and draw this fancy pink shaver
in long lines

like a snowplow
up my frightened legs.

FIRST DATE

Shaving must feel like this. A beard—promising.

This is before I know you.

Opening the medicine cabinet; foaming cream into your palm.

You joke with me at school—I like your voice.

You smooth it on. You take the razor

The doorbell rings! The door opens . . .

and bare your cheek . . .

we talk as we explore the pier . . .

Behold: your face.

THIS KISS

this time I know
it's me he likes
my mouth, my lips
my ooooh my

I taste tomato
and sourdough
and cold, sweet
pistachio

this time I *know*
it's so good to know
whoa
Carl-ooooooooooh

INVASION

He
swarms in my ribs.
Circling, clattering, buzzing, alive
inside me
without pause
a thousand bees
two thousand wings
bound by invisible threads
doubling in strength in my stomach and throat
filling the bones in my legs
behind my eyes
the roaring noise
takes over my insides.

I am a shell
to this second life
this surge
crashing against my skin
keeping me up all night.

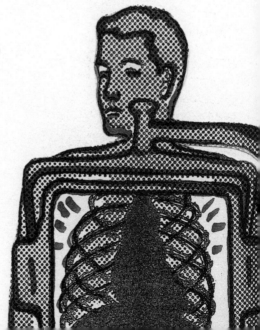

WHY CAN'T WE

why do we sit,
facing the blackboard,
your back to me?

why can't you
turn around,
mess up the papers?

why not
take all the day
in
one
    long
        kiss?

why can't we?

DRAMA PARTY

I'm wearing my new red dress
laughing with the drama crowd
beside Mr. J's pool.
I'm wearing my new red dress
excited
to be invited.

This is my first drama party
and I giggle as some of the guys toss
Meredith into the pool—she is laughing hysterically.
Then we sit down on lawn chairs for the annual awards.
My heart is high in my red dress.
Frank gets Best Actor, of course
and Meredith gets Best Actress (she really is).
She drips up the aisle and everyone laughs and so does she

and my heart is high.
I love being here.
Even Ox gets an award, I forget what
and then—then they call my name.
I can hardly believe it!
Frank and Meredith are at the microphone

I'm walking up the aisle in my red dress
when they announce my award:
the Susie Spineless Award.
I'm not hearing them.
It's dark, so they probably can't see my face
I am walking
I am smiling hard
in my new red dress.

BIRTHDAY

Deep in my closet,
crouched and crying
I know that something dark is coming.

"Slow it down,
lock it out,"
I sob.

Mama finds me,
rocks me, tells me,
"Growing up is wonderful—

you'll see,
you'll see."

All I want
is to be in her arms,
rocking.

ALARMED

An alarm
buried deep in me
rings
when you kiss me so hard.
When will it turn off?

SPACE   MAN

It's clear—
        looking at his punched-down brow—
he wants to be far,
far away.

"I think," I say, "you want to be at Frank's house,
not here
after school
with me."

His brow relaxes.
He rises to leave;
gently touches my bare foot
with his hard shoe.

He leaves,
clicking down
the school's stone steps
like a door snapped shut.

I drape my head
over my hands
and tuck my toes
as a soft wind cools the air.

It's safe to cry, now.

LANGUAGE ARTS—WRITING EXERCISE

"A writer,"
Mr. Barton says,
"writes."

*"But what if we don't feel like it
or we're too tired
or we have nothing to say?"*

"Then you write: 'I don't feel like writing.'
'I'm too tired.'
'I have nothing to say.'"

"For the whole page?"
"For the whole ten minutes.
Starting now."

Well, pooh on you, Mr. Barton. I don't feel like writing. I'm too
tired. I have nothing to say. I don't feel like writing. I'm too
tired. I have nothing to say. Nothing-nothing-nothing-nothing-
nothing-nothing-nothing-nothing-nothing-nothing to say-
nothing-nothing-nothing-nothing-nothing-nothing-nothing-
hahaha-nothing-nothing-nothing-nothing-nothing-nothing-
NOTHING-nothing-nothing-nothing-nothing-nothing-nothing-
pooh on you, Mr. Barton-nothing-nothing-nothing-nothing-
nothing-I hate Carlo I'm scared Good-bye.

DOWN BY THE DUCKS

there is something about this place.
I lean my bike against the grassy hill
and suck in the smell of
duck brown water

I walk across
wet grass
stuffing my jacket pockets
with cold hands

no one else
needs these ducks
needs this place
more than I

SAND CRAB

I stomp along the hard sand
that's been licked by the sea,

watching a little bird
search for sand crabs.

I want to yell,
"Hey, you!

Looking for a crab?
Look at me!"

HELICOPTER THOUGHT

I'm lying in bed
and here it comes
again:
my Helicopter Thought.

I'm a helicopter
pulling farther and farther away from the ground
until everyone seems
small

I see the big picture
and tiny little me
and the ripples in the land
that you can't see from down there

I'm looking at my small insignificant square
which from down there seemed so gigantic
one little piece of this huge expanse
this wide world made up of gazillions of squares

Higher and higher goes my helicopter
I see how my worries
are really small, really nothing
not when you look at them from here.

God bless my Helicopter Thought.

IT WAS NICE KISSING YOU

"Good-bye,"
I said.
"It was nice kissing you."

I just knew
that all the space in the world
wouldn't be enough for him

and as close as he could ever come
would never
be close enough for me.

SISTER / FRIEND

if I ever forget
how much you
feel
know
sense

may I remember
this April night
and you,
listening to my breaking voice
and blowing softly on my wet cheeks

MS. KONIGSBERG
TOLD ME IN CHORUS TODAY

that my throat
        opened on every note—
        my voice was strong
        as it soared up and out!

I popped right on top
        smack on top
        of each
        note!

No more
        breathy
        thin voice for me!
        Today I'm a singer.

Today I *sing*.

NO HIDING

I'm in school rush hour,
running to first period,
running up the quad steps behind Meredith,
thinking I should hide.

She's popular.
She doesn't like me.
Thinking I *could* hide.
No way.

No way out, is the plain truth.
So I just plant myself right here,
right here on these stone steps,
and bloom.

I bloom the bloomiest bloom in the whole county:
bright yellow and
happy
and loud as a waterfall at close range.

And I feel all charged up
and sparkly
and she just
            disappears.

COMING AROUND TO
YOUR POINT OF VIEW

I've come to where you were
after you've passed by.

I'm a block behind—
I look up just as you're turning

                                    the corner.

I'm now
where you were.

I see where your shoes bent this grass
where you stood between these two houses

looking back at me,
waiting.

PUBLISHED!

A letter in the mail!
They're going to PUBLISH my poem.
In their magazine.
In June.

My brain is exploding! I can't sleep!
I woke up early,
my body buzzy
like a playground ball boing-ing down a long hallway.

<<<THEY'RE GOING TO PUBLISH MY POEM!>>>
I won't tell anyone.
I'll wait until the magazine comes out.
How can I wait that long?

I won't tell anyone.
I'll just casually hand them the magazine
or wait
until someone at school sees it.

What will Carlo think?
What will Frank think?
What will Yen-Mei think?
What will Leslie think?????????

I won't tell anyone.
I won't tell anyone
and boy,
will they be surprised.

They're going to
publish my poem!
My poem! *My poem!*
Who can I call at 5:30 in the morning?

ME, CENTER OF THE UNIVERSE

If the whole world
Would just move
About two feet
To the right

Then I
Could see
The moon.

MY DAD LETTERED IN SPORTS

My dad is sitting in the TV room
on the rug against the couch
watching the last few seconds of the game.

His hands are behind his head.
His elbows are angled like a huge *W*.

His mouth is open too wide,
like a colossal *O*.

His legs are tense.
His bent knees look like a tremendous *N*.

My dad's body
is trying
to spell.

WELL-NAMED

"My name," says Great-Aunt Ida,
looking up from her sewing,
"is *idea*
without the *e*."
Then she goes back to sewing
the hat she just designed.

IN PRINT

One
Big
WOW
Fills my mouth.

DEBUT

Mr. Barton
reads it to the class
slowly, letting each line
linger.

Mr. Barton
reads it to the class
and I am
soaring—

over all the buildings
over all the people
I am a winged word
flying.

REVIEWS

Frank comes up, magazine in hand, laughing,
whacks me on the back and says,
"Amaz-a-lating! I didn't know you had it in you!"

Carlo smiles right into my eyes
and says, "Illiant-bray!"
Silly old bear.

Leslie
and Yen-Mei
bring balloons.

And Meredith? After school in drama,
she says to Frank, loud enough for me to hear,
"Yeah. That magazine publishes *anything*."

All those compliments. All that encouragement.
So why do I keep thinking about what Meredith said,
instead?

ALMOST SUMMER

on the cool grass
                of the park
                              in the dark

we sit talking
rolling our fingers over the moon
we sing and wave our legs
madly in the air

wonderfully tired
knowing no one needs us anywhere
we fall asleep
head to head

on the cool grass
                of the park
                              in the dark

SPRING FEVER

Fed up with this dull
class, my mind pecks open its
cage and flies away.

SISTER-SISTER-SISTER

If I didn't have a sister
and your all-encompassing call
If I didn't have your rich chocolate sweetness
                    your sun-going-down yes-ness
your ringingbat-fleetfeet-homerun-triumphantcheerleading
in my own stadium,

I don't know
I just don't know how I'd stand as tall,
sweep the dog hair from this sunny hall quite so snapping clean,
breathe in this honeysuckle flower,
or lean back, close my eyes,
and take in the shower steam.

Sister-sister-sister take this in:
there's nothing better than knowing
knowing inside me and outside in the high clouds, too,
that you are in this strange-wonderful-awful-justsilly place
this world with me.
Nothing better.

MONOPOLY

It's quiet in our kitchen, except for the dice
That my sneaky, scheming sister gets to toss out twice.

They rattle in her piggish fist, then spill across the board
My mom and dad and I watch as she adds to her hoard.

The evening wind blows soft—my favorite kind of weather
The light above the table seems to gather us together

I lie in wait, a sentinel
To see who lands on my hotels

Instead, Dad rolls, buys B. & O.
It's my turn next, I wish—then throw.

We jump to hear my mother wail.
It's her turn—she lands in jail.

The evening wind blows soft—my favorite kind of weather
The light above the table seems to gather us together

It's quiet in our kitchen, except for the dice . . .

ANGELS

One last hill in P.E.
Don't want to charge up it.
Too far.
Too steep.
Truth is, I'm not sure I can make it.

Yen-Mei and Leslie are in the crowd ahead.
I'm hurting inside and out—
wilting, nearly walking, close to giving up.
And then my two friends
           do the most astonishing thing.

They turn around and run back to me,
take my hands in theirs,
and we run
three across
up this last hard hill.

Race run. Race won.

COMING IN FOR A LANDING

My heart
is coming in
for a landing.

Carrying a suitcase
packed with hope.

I stuffed it,
sat on it to snap the clasps.

And as my heart dips from the cloud high
and slowly descends,

finally taxiing to the gate,
someone will unload my suitcase.

I am holding its tag tightly.
I have come to reclaim it.

Taking care . . .
taking it
home.

After Words

by April Halprin Wayland

A candle. That's what writing is for me. It lights up dark places in my life so that I can see them clearly. Writing poetry, usually late at night in my journal, is a way of sorting out emotions I can't express any other way.

Many of the poems in *Girl Coming In for a Landing* are from my journals. Some are the result of the kind of observation my poetry teacher, Myra Cohn Livingston, taught us. Don't just sit at your desk and try to remember what grass is like, she'd say. Go outside, look at it, smell it, feel it, lie down on it. *Then* write about grass.

Other poems are purely from my imagination. And although I've used the names of certain real people, most of the characters are composites. For instance, "Carlo" is the name of a man I once heard sing sea chanteys. I love the sound of that name. In this story, he's a combination of boys I had crushes on, actual boyfriends, and my husband. (I never did date the guy I had a crush on when I was a teen.)

Mr. C is not a composite. He's Charles Campman, my biology teacher at Santa Monica High School. An extraordinary educator, he often told stories that led into lessons, as in "Driving That Dog Crazy."

Another teacher told us to observe an animal, think of a human behavior that paralleled what it was doing, and then write a poem. I went down to the beach and watched seagulls flying in intersecting circles in the fog. A human parallel came to me right away: political leaders pointing fingers at underlings, who were pointing fingers at leaders, with no one taking responsibility for the events of that time.

"This should be published!" my teacher wrote on that poem. I raced home and sent it off to *McCall's* magazine. I'm not sure why I picked *McCall's*. My family didn't subscribe to it. Maybe it seemed like the kind of magazine other people subscribed to.

Every day I checked the mail. Weeks went by. Finally, many months later, *McCall's* sent an impersonal rejection. I was crushed. I didn't submit anything for *fifteen* years.

I wish someone had given me guidance, helping me find a magazine that published poetry by teens. That's why I continue to update the list "Where Can a Young Writer Get Published?" on my Web site (www.aprilwayland.com). For writers like you.

If you want to write and be published, try this:

- Read. Read to escape. Read for inspiration. When you don't know how to say what you want to say, search for a poem you love. Then imitate its pattern. Fit your idea into that form.

- Use all five senses. Observe yourself, a bird, the scuffed curb, how someone prepares food, opens a door, or plays guitar. Crumble a leaf in your fist. How does root beer feel going down?

- Live! Play! Be a little crazy. Take a few deep breaths. *Be present*.

- Write in your journal. Even if it's just for one minute. Describe one memorable thing. Take a day or two off from writing each week.

- Then *make a mess*. Throw all your raw material onto the page and see what sticks. It doesn't have to be good. It just has to be words.

- Now close in on your topic. Focus. Eliminate distractions (unneeded words, other ideas). Include specific details you've observed. Rearrange the words. Play with them on the page. Rewrite like crazy.

Take your time.

- When it's ready, read it aloud. Does it work? Send it out.

- If you get rejected, don't wait fifteen years, as I did. Take a fresh look at it. Revise it. Send it out again. Don't give up. I'll tell you a secret—this book was rejected by publishers for *ten years* before it was finally accepted.

Not yet ready for (or interested in) publication? That's okay. Plenty of people write but don't want to be published. Or they want to be published, but not yet. Maybe you just love to write. Maybe it helps you sort out your thoughts and feelings.

Writing's my way of sorting out emotions I don't know how to express any other way. It will always be my candle in the dark.

May it be your candle, too.

April Halprin Wayland
another late night
Los Angeles, California

WILLIAM SHAKESPEARE'S
"SONNET NUMBER TWELVE"

When I do count the clock that tells the time,
And see the brave day sunk in hideous night;
When I behold the violet past prime,
And sable curls all silvered o'er with white;
When lofty trees I see barren of leaves
Which erst from heat did canopy the herd,
And summer's green all girded up in sheaves
Borne on the bier with white and bristly beard,
Then of thy beauty do I question make,
That thou among the wastes of time must go,
Since sweets and beauties do themselves forsake
And die as fast as they see others grow;
And nothing 'gainst Time's scythe can make defense
Save breed, to brave him when he takes thee hence.

Shakespeare, William. "Sonnet No. 12." *The Norton Anthology of English Literature: The Major Authors*. M. H. Abrams, editor. New York: W. W. Norton & Company, 1987.

"Taking Violin," "Those School Dances," "My Father Whistles the Hills," "Duet," "Procrastination," "Grand Central Market, Los Angeles," and "My Dad Lettered in Sports" first published in *Cricket* magazine.

Index